CW01269980

WHAT DARKNESS COVERS

What Darkness Covers

Tony Curtis

Arc
PUBLICATIONS
2003

Published by Arc Publications
Nanholme Mill, Shaw Wood Road
Todmorden, Lancs OL14 6DA, UK

Copyright © Tony Curtis 2003

Design by Tony Ward
Printed by Antony Rowe Ltd.,
Eastbourne, East Sussex, UK

ISBN 1 900072 53 X

Acknowledgements are due to the editors of the following where some of these poems appeared for the first time:

The Irish Times, Poetry Ireland Review, Equinox, Portal (EXPO 2000), *Force 10, An Táin* (Melbourne), *Irish Scene* (Perth), *The Journal* (Perth), *The Stinging Fly, The Bloomsday Magazine.*

Many of these poems have been broadcast on *RTÉ Radio, Lyric FM, Anna Livia and Talk Radio FM106.*

'Juliet Sleeping' appeared in *The Write Stuff* English & Media Studies for Transition Year edited by Martin Kieran and Frances Rocks; 'Masterplan' appeared in *The Living Stream: A Festschrift for Theo Dorgan* edited by Niamh Morris; 'The Boat' appeared in *Out To Lunch*, an anthology published by the Bank of Ireland and edited by John McNamee; 'Another Room' appeared in English and Flemish in *De Brakke Hond* (Belgium) edited by Nessa O'Mahony; 'Nude', 'Big', 'Blind' and 'Panic' appeared in *The Clifden Anthology* edited by Brendan Flynn. 'Currach' was set to music by the Irish composer Ian Wilson.

The author gratefully acknowledges The Arts Council, Ireland / An Chomhairle Ealaíon for a generous grant which helped kick start this book.

Cover illustration by Liam McGowan
Cover design by Pat Mooney

The publishers acknowledge financial assistance from the Arts Council of England, Yorkshire

Editor, UK & Ireland: Jo Shapcott

For Mary and Oisín

*and to the memory of
Michael Hartnett
gone with the autumn leaves.*

CONTENTS

Blind / 11
What Darkness Covers / 12
Another Room / 14
Juliet Sleeping / 15
Nude / 16
The Long Rest / 18
Masterplan / 19
Currach / 21
Invisible Mending / 23
Still Life With Books / 24
Baffled / 25
Small Interior / 28

Three Found Poems
1. *The Weight Of The World* / 33
2. *One Hundred* / 34
3. *Sister* / 35

Lemon Tree / 36
Lemon Cake / 37

Asylum
1. *Tears* / 38
2. *Company* / 38
3. *As Into A Well* / 39
4. *I Miss You* / 39

Thirteen / 40
Trowel / 41

Gallery: twelve poems after paintings by Lucian Freud
1. *Portrait* / 45
2. *Nude With Legs* / 47
3. *Caroline With White Dog* / 48
4. *Dark Chocolate* / 49
5. *Big* / 50
6. *December Light* / 52
7. *Woman On A Quay* / 53
8. *Self-Portrait* / 54
9. *Girl In Bed* / 55
10. *Naked Girl With Egg* / 56
11. *The Bateman Sisters* / 57
12. *Male Nudes* / 58

Critic / 59
The Boat / 60
Nine Lines About Love / 61
Into The Dark / 62
Snowlines / 64
Cactus With Stuffed Lizard / 67
Petrarch's Wife / 69
Panic / 70
Mountain Woman / 71
Jimmy / 73
The Olympians / 74
Now Winter's Over / 78

Four Remedies:
1. *Cure For The Broken Hearted* / 79
2. *Cure For Melancholia* / 81
3. *Cure For Excess Of Wine* / 83
4. *Cure For Loneliness* / 84

About the author / 87

All of old. Nothing else ever. Ever tried. Ever failed. No matter. Try again. Fail again. Fail better.

Worstward Ho – Samuel Beckett

*Tonight my love's eyes
are the colour of the sea
and I wish to drown.*

It is way past midnight.

*I am writing
by lamp light, darkness
lapping at my feet.*

BLIND

Now when I call, she says,
"Step close and let me see you."
She lifts her fingers onto my face,
then up over my eyes so I go blind.

I smell the lavender on her hands,
the ash in the grate, cat smells, church smells,
turf and apple-mint. An apron hung to dry.
The smell of the yard on boots by the door.

And beyond the door, the weather:
rain and mist. Earth-smells:
cattle and woodburn. The dead leaves
at the dead end of the year. And all

through the wood, the whirling wind,
the open wing, eggshell and birdsong,
and mosses from the riverbank
smelling of frog and flick of fish tail.

Then, as she lifts her fingers
releasing my eyes back into the light,
"You're looking well," she says,
and asks for news of weather and the day.

WHAT DARKNESS COVERS

Because I cannot sleep
and you are far away,
this dishevelled bed
holds no dreams,
and blankets and darkness
cover only emptiness.
I look where you should be
but you are utterly gone.
I lie remembering.

My grandmother used to say
the dead love this time of year,
the nights so long
they walk amongst us whispering.
This morning I found
footprints on the path,
tears on every leaf.
*Listen, is that a door opening
or a door closing?*

Old Italians used to say
the most beautiful sculpture
Michelangelo ever made
was a snowman
in the Boboli Gardens:
a male nude chiselled out of ice,
you could see where his soul
was held. He turned all to tears
and was washed away.

I do this all the time,
try to hold on.
Sometimes I feel
I am the last leaf on the tree,
and there will be no rest
until I fall. So I say –
Let everything that falls, fall,
beginning with tired love
and ending in the old way:

the eyes still,
the breath gone,
all quiet until
the earth's rain falls.

ANOTHER ROOM

This was our room,
it has four walls,
I counted them
when you left:

The one with the door,
the one with our pictures,
the one with the window,
the one with our bed.

But now, to put away the memory
of how your hands, your mouth
turned my skin into electricity,
I have taken myself away.

I have moved to another room.
It too has four walls,
but the door opens to the other side,
and there are no pictures of you.

And in the dark,
when I bury your ghost,
the memory of your touch
goes out with the light.

JULIET SLEEPING

Unused to a baby
in the house,
the grandmother
has emptied turf
from a creel
and filled it with
soft cotton sheets.
Now Juliet sleeps
in a wicker bed,
dreaming of moss.

"And not just moss,"
the grandmother says,
"but all of the woods,
the light and the half-light,
for it is late autumn
and this child is dreaming
the brown into her eyes."

NUDE

She has been with me all winter.
I cannot say I hate her
for when I was young
I loved everything about her.
There were nights
I could have died for her.
Now there's an awful
pattern to our lives.

She arrives late September
carrying sacks of old books,
and pinned to her dress
or tied in her hair,
or buried in the folds
of her skin,
are those few new poems
I have waited all summer to hear.

But each year her price
goes a little higher
and I grow weary.
Often she undresses
to the bone:
peeling her skin,
folding the wrinkled
hide over the bed
where she sups and stares.

Often she strips me too,
planting the tips
of her fingers
like roots in my eyes,
or pushing her tongue
deep into my mouth.
Bare. Naked. Nude –
unless you've ever
served her,
felt her cunning
on your lips,
you'll never know
the meaning of the word.

And yet,
one of these mornings
I'll find her
standing in the kitchen
dressed for the road,
coat, hat, scarf,
bags tied with string,
and I'll be on my knees
begging her to stay.

THE LONG REST

Late autumn. They are taking the dead
from the church and bringing them
up to the field at the back of the town
where they will leave them forever.

It has put me in mind of the day
my grandfather retired.
Kathleen and Carmel, the daughters
who lived with him at home,

had cooked rashers and sausages,
baked sweet apple tart, had the
kettle on the stove, ready to scald
the leaves when they heard the gate.

Half-past-six, the same as every other day,
the latch was lifted, the bicycle stored
and my grandfather came in from work
to rest by the fireside forever.

He took from his waistcoat the silver
pocket watch he had been given,
told the girls he'd done well,
then gave them each a brown envelope.

Vouchers for Clery's?
Tickets to the Olympia?
No, my grandfather
was a practical man.

He had bought them a place in the shade
of a yew, up at the back of the town,
a bed for the long rest –
for each daughter, a grave.

MASTERPLAN

God made today
as he will make tomorrow,
as he made yesterday.

He has been doing this,
year in, year out,
for as long as I can remember.

The only thing he changes
is the weather
and how he moves

the people under the clouds:
some he brings into the world,
some he takes away.

He works magic with flowers,
miracles with water,
sorcery with stars.

He does this and that
and hallelujahs,
and bucketfuls of sadness.

What he does with love
and hate is a *tour-de-force:*
in a moment he can

break or mend your heart.
He assures us in his book
he has a masterplan,

that every step is neatly mapped
from the sorrow of whale song,
to the shyness of the platypus.

But all I want from him
is to slow
the whole thing down

so I can at least appreciate
all the work he has put in,
covering up the cracks.

CURRACH

This is my boat.
I made it
with my own hands.
I took salt
from a bitter wind,
hair from
a horse's mane,
thread from
a woman's blouse.

Three stories
my father told me.
The sideways look
my mother has
when she is
curious and alone.
Her silent prayers.
A few rusty nails
from the kitchen door.

Three views of the island:
one in mist, one in rain,
one rocking in a drunken sea.
No flowers.
My people
had no love of leaves,
they saw boats in trees;
now the boats are gone
and the hills are bare.

At night, I sowed
curses into the oars,
rubbed fish oil

into the wood,
for I knew the journey
that lay ahead.
My people's story
was written on water.
Most of it is washed away.

My grandfather
knew the tale
but he'd not tell it.
His ghost sits
in the stern
saying:

*"The future
is a steady course,
row strongly."*

INVISIBLE MENDING

They put me in the bed
where she died and I dreamt
again her last sad dream:

A woman is coming from a well
there is frost in the air
shards of ice in the water.

She is trying to remember
an old remedy
that is good for the breathing

and a stitch her mother taught her,
that will not show
when she takes in her dresses.

It is the morning before the birth
of her first child. If you listen,
you can hear her footsteps.

As I awoke, they died away.

STILL LIFE WITH BOOKS

Most mornings I wake early
as if I have somewhere to go,
something to do. I potter
for an hour through books,
papers, photographs.

Then I sit by the window
for the rest of the day.

And if there is rain,
I fish for tears.
And if there is mist,
I sift for ghosts.
And if there is snow,
I chisel for stars.

In between
I pace the room
or watch the gate
for the comfort
of the postman. How
did I end up like this?

A watcher of skies
and fields that run to clouds;
a keeper of stillness,
a moonface at the window,
a love gone to darkness,
a still life with books.

BAFFLED

Like you, I have spent
most of my life baffled.
No sooner does the light
dawn than it's dark again.
There are times I wonder
why I get out of bed
to traipse the streets
like a familiar ghost
heading for the fruit market.
How can bananas
become somebody's life?

And before this,
when I lived in the
grave-digger's cottage,
she said my skin
always smelt of the dead.
Six feet down,
level with their bones,
I could hear them sighing.
Mid-winter, I'd swear
their eyes were watching.
Fewer died over Christmas,
most panted on until
the new year, gave
out crossing the line.
*What did you get
for Christmas? A grave.*

The Parish Priest
would call down
"Make sure you
square the edges.
Nothing settles out

a life better than
a smooth descent."
His own went as easily
as the tide turning.
I can still remember
my surprise at how
upset she was. As they
lowered the coffin
she began to cry.
I thought at first
it was a seagull.

Living close to the shore
they were always on at me
to go to sea. But though
I loved an old dip, the sea
is something else
that has always baffled me:
it goes up, it goes down.
It comes in, it goes out,
like a drunk's friendship
with his favourite bar.
And then for no reason
other than a freshening breeze
or a scrap of cloud,
it flies into a rage
and spits stones.
Bad weather, and the boats
could be tied up for weeks.
If you want me, I'll be in the bar.
Strange that when you are young
she lies before you
like a floozie.

You suck and swallow
suck and swallow
until thirty years later
you stare across
the table at the shadow
keeping you company
and say, *"One of these days
I must give this up."*
He laughs and gets in
another round
and the world spins on…

We live for what we love
and wait for death.
Surely love and death
are the two great shrines
to the bewildered.
I am a disciple of one
heading towards the other,
bothered that life
is not a tightrope
along which we edge
in our own creaky fashion,
but something tossed away
by a famished god,
a banana skin awaiting
the heel of another
hapless pilgrim.

SMALL INTERIOR

> *If you wandered through a poet's*
> *brain you would not see poetic*
> *thoughts there.*
> — Gwen Harwood

☙

The room I write in has an oak door, a wooden floor, a well of book shelves, a window and a table where I sit with my back to the light. On the walls around me are the postcards, small greetings from wandering souls. A quick glance and I see Puccini, Beckett, a study of a naked woman posing on a chair. There are paintings by Picasso, Gauguin, Bacon, Mattise; Chagall's wedding is pinned up and Schiele's *Reclining Woman*. I found her in the V&A.
Wish you were here!

☙

I've one, two, three, four nudes by Lucian Freud; cards from London's New Tate. And from Paul in Liverpool, not the Beatles or the Mersey, but lots of Edward Hopper: late-night bars where men in coats sip bourbon – any one of them could be Dylan Thomas, circa 1953. And he's up there too, painted by Augustus John, the big man who painted the poet's wife. She used to say he took her on the studio floor.
Everything's so cheap!

༃

There's a card from Istanbul, a map of the old city – wouldn't that be Byzantium? There's a photo of me standing by the Bosphorus taken the day I took a taxi from Asia to Europe. And there's a great photo of you naked on a beach in Australia reading Judith Wright's poems, the ocean behind you so blue.
Weather's lovely!

༃

There are Tibetan mandalas beside irreverent cartoons. There are invitations to launches, invitations to tea, rejections, receipts, notes, bills. And dotted between them is a sprinkling of islands: the Blaskets, the Orkneys, the Shetlands, Crete, Tasmania, Sicily. How are they formed? Does the earth rise or the water recede? Someone told me that Everest was once at the bottom of the ocean, and climbers close to the top often find shells. I wonder do they still hold the sound of the sea?
The beach is beautiful!

Only two of the cards are in black and white: Bob Dylan travellin' through Balbriggan station on his way to play Belfast in the summer of '65 and a John Minihan photo of a duffel-coated Beckett drinking coffee, smoking a cheroot and waiting for someone. Was he ever photographed in summer? Minihan has frozen him forever in a polo-neck and duffel.

I'm practically naked all day!

This morning a card arrived from Jack in Berlin, another nude: a German woman photographed in 1935. I wonder how she fared in the war? I'll put her up there close to the ceiling, out of harm's way, between a poster by the Mexican painter Alfonso Lopez Monreal and a picture of a Cistercian monastery at Tarrawarra, in the Yarra valley, about forty miles outside Melbourne. My uncle Paul was a monk there; I got it when I visited the monastery last year.

So peaceful and quiet!

℘

A spring morning, the monks brought me out to the small graveyard where Paul is buried under a simple iron cross. They showed me the church where he prayed, the shed where he mended things; sat me in his old truck and sang the first verse of his favourite song. They said he sang it when he drove the sheep to the market in Melbourne, Gene Autry's *South of the Border Down Mexico Way*. N.D.A was printed on the truck's door and when the farmers or the bushmen asked him what it stood for, he'd declare "No dames allowed!".

Still on my own!

℘

Each card is a dream filter, a small bell that chimes in my soul. If I had to choose one for Desert Island Discs, I'd choose the nude of you on that beach in Australia. But I suppose that would be like taking Shakespeare or the Bible. So I'd go with either Billie Whitelaw in *Happy Days* or William Orpen's *Sunlight*.

It's pretty as a picture here!

☙

Apart from this morning's post, my latest acquisitions are *The Death of Culture* by the American model and photographer Lee Miller, and an unforgettable photograph of her soaking in Hitler's bath during the last days of war. I bought them in Edinburgh. I pinned them either side of Gary Snyder's 'What You Should Know To Be A Poet'. I love that poem, its great last line: "real danger. gambles. and the edge of death".

I could happily die here!

☙

Looking round my room I sometimes think that this is what it must be like inside my head: a higgle of postcards held up by ghosts, a thousand images falling like rain, a patchwork, a shadowland of ifs and buts. Of who is she? And who is he? And when and where was that? And then, when I close my eyes to look more closely there is always only the same small black and white self-portrait of me; it's untitled, but I call it:

Nude, in small interior

THREE FOUND POEMS

1. The Weight of the World

An old woman in the market asks
the fishmonger for a pound of kippers.

"Sorry love," he says,
"we only do kilos now."

"Alright so," she says
"a pound of kilos please."

2. One Hundred

> *A man on the radio talks*
> *about being 100 years old*

"I met her when she was seventeen.
She used to sing in the Choir;
one of those voices close to angels.

She was always younger than me.
A small, beautiful woman,
she turned heads on the street

and my heart on the pillow.
Dead seven years now, seven dead
years – I sleep with her ghost.

I put this long life
down to taking time
to make and drink, love and tea."

3. Sister

from the newspaper

My feet are the hardest to keep warm.
It takes me eight minutes to walk
from my cell, through the copse
and walled garden, up to the monastery.
I go to the house for eight o'clock mass.
I meet Sister Theresa in the kitchen
and read the obituaries in yesterday's paper.
She gives me my basket of food for the day:
bran, vegetables, Ryvita, cheese, apples.
I allow myself four crisps each evening;
a small packet lasts me the whole week.
I drink a lot of coffee, you see the sisters
buy it in vast cartons to help the Third World.
When I've finished with the lists of the dead,
I shuffle back through the garden to my cell
where I won't see or talk to anyone until
the next morning. I read military history,
biographies, art books, novels, a little poetry,
and, of course, the Bible – the psalms mostly.
When I came to live in solitude, I decided
I would spend five hours in prayer
for each two at work or rest. Prayer is God's
world, you just have to hold yourself
to enter his land. At sixty-eight, it's a great
disappointment that I'm too old to die young.
Death is a supreme act of faith. I hope that
when it comes I will have long enough to say
"Yes!" so that I can welcome death.
Before bed, I put my feet in lovely hot water.
I'm very tired when I say, "It is you, O Lord,
who are my happiness." When I sleep,
I cover myself in the word of God.

LEMON TREE

Christmas in Melbourne,
and there is a lemon tree
at the back of the house.

In all my life I could not
use so many lemons:
all those coughs and colds,

all those gin and tonics,
all those dreary salads,
all that sweet bitterness.

It is so hot here now
I have spent all afternoon
in its sandy shade

imagining you here,
dressed only in an open kimono,
the wind revealing you

to me at her will
as I sip sweet tea,
the little moons of lemon,

like this
abandoned love,
bitter to the end.

LEMON CAKE

Sometimes
when you stand
shadowed in a dusty light,

I am three years old
again, in the middle pew
of a grey, tin church.

Head squirmed round,
eyes watching the door
for my mother to catch up.

She'd come
out of the sunlight
into the land of sorrow.

And all through mass,
I'd sit quietly
holding her hand.

For that
there would be
lemon cake.

ASYLUM

1. Tears

No one in their right mind
stays in the building where
the tears of the world are held,
but I walk through the rain
past the clock tower
the water tower
the laundry tower
the mortuary,
everything exactly as it was
the last time I sallied
only closer to the edge:
the gutters leak, the windows weep,
the flowerbeds are tarmacadam.
Folly to think it would be any other way.

2. Company

This is all I know, I am here today;
if I look in the mirror I will see
a middle-aged man, hair going grey,
falling around a face that resembles me:
the sunken mouth, the same dark eyes.
When I turn away, he turns away
but I have no idea where he goes
for he does not come with me.
Besides, he is poor company.
Nothing to say. Quiet as a mouse.
I never even hear him scream or cry
at the other end of the house.
So I often sigh, just to let him know
I'm here in the dark. I would not go.

3. As Into A Well

You left your soul with me
when you went away.
Now I read to her, talk to her,
tell her things I'd never say to you;
that my heart aches while you're away.
I tend to her, sleep with her,
for without you this empty house
fills with ghosts and all the dust returns.

4. I Miss You

The bathroom has come into the kitchen
and the kitchen has come into the bedroom.
And the bedroom and the kitchen and the
bathroom have all come into the living room.
And the attic, the hall, the landing and the
stairs are all crammed into the front porch.
The garden's run wild, it has captured the path
and is holding the drive to ransom.
In truth, my whole world has shifted:
there are weeds growing out of the teapot,
and I seem to be keeping the bed in the fridge,
or the fridge in the bed. I now know
what you mean about dust. I miss you,
but first I need to set everything straight.

THIRTEEN

A dark number
blamed for the darkest times.
Step under it, step over it,
step round it, step away from it.
The worst year of childhood: finished,
done with, locked away until
death's door slamming opens it again.
A cardinal number coming after twelve.
A baker's dozen. A coven. The witching hour
when the roof rattles, the walls creak
and the water shivers in the pipes.

>   Thirteen ruffled feathers
>   Thirteen bells tolling for no one
>   Thirteen tuneless songs
>   Thirteen lines of prayer
>   Thirteen dead leaves
>   falling through the autumn sky…

Thirteen months in the year
those extra few weeks squeezed
between November and December
when the clocks lose an hour
and the world spins into darkness.
When time opens and thirteen witches,
their brooms, their cats,
their cackles and their spells,
fall in on me. It's cramped.
But you, neighbour, banging on the wall,
can't imagine the triskaidekaphobia
going on inside Number Thirteen.

TROWEL

after Allen Ginsberg

I have seen the best minds of my generation destroyed by DIY.

GALLERY

Twelve Poems after Paintings
by Lucian Freud

1. Portrait

There are naked portraits
and naked portraits,
but this
is a truly naked portrait.

One of my knees is up
so high it covers my breast,
the other is spread
to open me like a flower.

Curled on a bed,
I could be a woman
who has just given birth,
the loss still on her face.

Or I might be a baby
in the womb –
writhing like a fish,
slithering for the first time.

Or maybe I am
a captured soul,
tortured and abused,
a victim, somebody's prey.

But then, spread
on this white sheet
I might as easily be an Eskimo
listening at an ice-hole

for a seal's breath.
Or in my skin, a seal
under the ice, listening
for an Eskimo's footsteps.

Or maybe I am simply
what I seem, a woman
on a bed after love-making –
neither here nor there –

her man, trailing excuses,
gone to make tea and toast.
The only thing I'm certain of
is I am changed:

painted like this, it is
as if my soul
has been branded,
tattooed, nailed to the wall.

2. Nude With Legs

A nude woman
sits in an attic door
legs dangling above
a confession box,
basking in sinshine.

3. Caroline With White Dog

I

Someone told me that in later years
she married the poet Robert Lowell,
the one who died in a yellow taxi cab.
Here Caroline rests on a low sofa,
with a white dog sleeping on her lap.
The room looks quiet as a mortuary.
Through her open yellow robe
one beautiful white breast is held
like an offering to an invisible child
or the ghost of the poet. For who
can tell what she saw as she posed,
her two eyes wide open to the future?

II

This morning I looked at the painting again
and for the first time I noticed the birth-
mark on her hand and realised
it was not Caroline at all, but Kitty,
the painter's first wife, looking cold
and exposed; guarding her frail soul.

When I pointed this out to you over breakfast,
you said you'd always known that it was Kitty,
just as you'd always known the white dog
was a wedding present, one of a pair.
The other was completely black and was
in fact the dog chosen for the painting.
It was run over by a car, so the black pelt
was changed to white. Everything second best.

4. Dark Chocolate

Here's how I like it:
sweet, melted over nipples,
mouthfuls at a time.

5. Big

It wasn't that I was always big.
It wasn't that at four years of age
I began eating only doughnuts.

It's something in me:
an old ache, not heartache,
but something like neglect.

The year would turn
and every summer
I'd be bigger than before.

And then this man
stops me in the street
saying he'd like to paint me, nude.

Pervert, I thought
and so old
with mean eyes,

skinny as a whippet.
I asked him to leave me alone
or take himself back to the home.

But a week later he called to my hatch –
I'm a benefit supervisor –
with photos of his work.

They were nothing like I'd seen
before: men and women naked
but dressed; living in their skin.

Six months I sat for him
in his studio
on the Marylebone Road.

Now I'm up on the wall
in the New Tate,
for everyone to see.

When I go to see myself
people always point
and the guard winks.

I sometimes wonder
what my mother
would have made of me.

I suppose she wouldn't
have minced her words.
But I think, naked

I look glorious.
Look at me:
I look like a woman

taking a bath without water.
A saint burning without flames.
A bird opening its wings.

I look through a painter's eyes.
I look like I never looked before,
and yet, exactly the same.

6. December Light

Last night the North Star
was so bright it has stolen
most of the light from the
morning sky and left it grey.

The model's skin looks cold
as ice. When he lifts his
arms above his naked body
I see pages of white vellum:

a monk by a monastery window
scribing the annals in green ink
drawn from holly. Beside him
a cat is sleeping by a log fire.

And though there is no snow,
it must be close to Christmas
for he is humming a carol so old
I know it is from another world.

7. Woman On A Quay

Thirteen centuries
of tired sailors tied up here;
mine loves our brass bed.

Nothing as sweet as
watching him bucking the waves,
parting the pillows.

He left with the tide.
I wait by the bitter sea –
empty as my bed.

8. Self-Portrait

Genghis Khan must have appeared
to early Christians as I do to you:
too real for prayer,
too wild to turn your back upon.

But this naked barbarian,
wearing only boots
stolen from a tramp,
offers you safe passage past.

Though I despise the way
some of you gape at me,
comparing your cocks to mine,
to each one of you I say, "Beware".

Do not think I have forgotten this.
There are rivers of nakedness behind me,
gouged from men and women,
starting with their eyes.

9. Girl In Bed

All the time I was drinking the coffee
I felt she was naked beneath the duvet.
The noise of traffic below was a distraction.
I wanted to close the high windows
but she was smoking French cigarettes
and looking for wine.
When she turned in the bed
I could see that her shoulders were bare.
I asked if she had ever been painted.
She said she didn't have the time.
And besides, she's seen them
up in Montmartre begging for faces.

10. Naked Girl With Egg

Up to this he always painted me
as just a naked model upon a sheet.

But a while ago he began adding
two fried eggs (sunny side up).

I thought he was enjoying a joke;
the eggs so similar to my breasts.

As he painted it dawned on me,
the eggs were my ovaries;

all I meant to him
was the cold white dish.

11. The Bateman Sisters

Fremantle, Western Australia

Between the red flowers and the yellow flowers,
in a garden as long and warm as last December,
the Bateman sisters sunbathe nude. They do this
every sunny day, and here every day is sunny.
Eva is twenty-one or two and Bella, with the
mauve birthmark on her breast, a little older.

Pablo Neruda and Robert Graves
would have rejoiced in them as muses;
Lucian Freud would have brought
their souls to the edge of their skin;
Rodin, moulded them in bronze;
Andy Warhol, canned them.

So what it is in me that cannot celebrate
their beauty, that looking out this window
feels only disquiet and regret?
The grey pieties of a damp, grey island.
I'd love to write a poem about how natural,
how beautiful the Bateman sisters are.

But I cannot get away from that boy
trapped in the coldness
of a Christian Brother's classroom:
All flesh is sin.
Your body is a temple.
A woman's curves are the Devil's tools.

To write unfettered by the Indian Ocean
in the heat of this blue day
I'd need to undress
And shed a lifetime of Irish rags.

12. Male Nudes

I enter the next room.

*Eleven naked carcasses
crucified on the wall —
I undress like an apostle;
cross over the threshold.*

CRITIC

> Vladimir: You should have been a poet.
> Estragon: I was. (*Gesture towards his rags.*)
> Isn't that obvious?
>
> Samuel Beckett

What I admire in this new collection
are the blank three pages at the back,
their pristine silence shows the lack
in everything that went before:
pages of stylish tosh,
twaddle of love and loss –
my greatest grief being the poet's
rhyming of Hecuba with vagina.
In a sequence of banal domestic sonnets
a dying father does everything but die –
God spare I spawn a poet as an heir.
After wading through the mire of profane
vapid verbiage that passes for 'modern verse',
it's the epilogue, the triptych that is sublime.
These blank pages stand like gravestones
for the dead Goddesses of verse,
Calliope, Erato, Euterpe,
lately buried by their sister Melpomene,
while the coffin-maker and the grave-digger
stole Medusa's magic from poems like these.

THE BOAT

Now that I have come this far there is no
    turning back.
And yet, what if there is nothing at the end
    of the track?

What if there is only more rock and sea?
    What if when
you open your eyes there's still the interminable
    grey rain?

Will you take it out on me? Or will you say,
    let us make our bed here.
Winter approaches and we need food
    and shelter.

For even in this emptiness we have each other.
    We are from the same mould,
close as body and soul, feather and air, fish
    and water, rain and wind.

And brushing the hair from your face, will you
    take my hand and place it on
your breast saying: How were you to know
    the boats would leave so soon?

How were you to know the boats were here at all?
    So, let me settle.
Cities have been built by men like you,
    waiting for the boat home.

NINE LINES ABOUT LOVE

Tossed pillows and crumpled white sheets
are snow covered mountains around you.
Light falls over your bare shoulders.

Nothing in this house as quiet as you sleeping.
We are a long way from home. You open your eyes
and your gaze is a lake I dipped my hand into long ago.

As I touched the skin of the water a fish leapt,
and I was suddenly caught in a ripple, as its soul
lifted my soul into the blue of the morning.

INTO THE DARK

i.m. Michael Hartnett (1941-1999)

It was a Wednesday
the thirteenth of October
a blue winter morning.
I walked the lanes
over the hill of Howth,
had breakfast by the sea,
wrote letters, bits of poems.
All this before the house
came tumbling in:

not by curse or magic
venom or lie
wizard or warlock
storm or blaze
but by pure dark –
Paula rang to say
"Michael is dead."

For years I'd watched him
sacrifice his old-age to poems.
I know they'll tell me
he'll live on in them,
that when I open his books
birds will flutter from the pages,
otters scurry from the riverbank,
prayers open like leaves,
old voices fill the air –
his cigarette smoke will curl
round me like a lonely ghost.

But tonight I feel it is not true,
for I can go nowhere to meet him,
the streets are all heartbreak.
His eyes and his voice are gone;
the voice that nailed
his poems in the air.

Watch for him tonight, O Lord,
you'll know him by his light.

SNOWLINES

Compared to this island
Valentia is a tea cosy,
Spitsbergen a metropolis.

Did you know the word 'Inuit'
means 'eater of raw meat'?
    I didn't.

I have been here a year now
and the worst of it is I feel
like St. Kevin in the wilderness.

Exhausted sea birds rest for days
when they arrive, closing their eyes
against the bitter north wind.

Grey seals, who love the emptiness,
sing; any time now
I'll be joining in all out of tune:

'Oh, I'm sailin' away my own true love,
I'm sailin' away in the morning.'

❦

This is a land that has lost its memory.
Even the hills have forgotten the trees.
Only tufts of grass remember green.
The rest is grey. I stand in the rain,
a wet hood tight around my face,
remembering ash settling on the fire;
smoke flicker as you'd come into the room
naked from a bath, drying your hair
with a towel. I miss your wet footprints
on the wooden floor, the warmth
of your voice, your soft brown eyes.

❦

Sometimes it gets so lonely here
I follow a disused mining track
a mile or two into the hills
to where some poor soul, long
forgotten, has strung a fence
up to the lake and abandoned mine.

It wasn't until it began to snow
that I realised the fence was a guideline
back to the jetty for the old miners
when snowstorms covered the land.

Maybe there's a photograph
on somebody's mantelpiece:
"Michael by the snowline.
Winter of '41"

Every morning I ask myself
'What am I doing here?'
You see, I had planned,
as poets do, to sit by a window
disturbed only by snow
and to make poems
out of the whiteness.
But alone, I lost the need.

Instead, I'm fluent in penguin,
and learning seal songs.
What I've really missed
are not papers or books,
but a settling in my soul.
I've missed you, your garden
and its sway of flowers.

So I've taken fence posts and earth
and made my own garden
at the back of the house.
In the centre of it all,
I've stuck your photograph
in an upturned glass –
the one I took of you in Australia.
Soon I'll have wild thyme
and rock roses coming into bloom.
Already, snowdrops and crocuses
are about to unfurl.

As for the poetry:
this is another plan
that has gone all wrong.

CACTUS WITH STUFFED LIZARD

There are things I know nothing about:
astrophysics, thermal reactors, gardening.
Elderflowers sound like old daisies to me;
herbaceous borders, places to avoid.
All my life I've wondered about seeds
and bulbs. Snowdrops, crocuses,
yellow daffodils – what is it
brings them back each year?

I know all there is to know about fountain pens
and staplers, but trees and flowers
are silicon and quantum mechanics to me.
Sometimes I find myself wondering:
How can they do what they do?
Blossom in season. Release all their leaves…

I know that cacti, coming from deserts, need little rain.
And yet, of all the flowers, shrubs, trees –
I don't even know which they are – they
unsettle me most. When I enter a room
with a cactus on a table,
I always feel an unbearable sadness.
I would release every cactus back into the desert
let them dry into the setting sun like withered old men.

I could make a list from here to the sea
of the things I know nothing about.
But this I do know: I am well over forty,
and though I still read and write,
I know less and less each passing year.
I used to know all about Beckett, bicycles,
beekeeping, The Book Of Chronicles,
Debussy, The Domesday Book…
but ask me now and we might as well
be discussing plant life along the Mississippi.

If I live to be eighty or eighty-one,
I will probably end up as sad and dry
as one of those horny, thick-skinned lizards
who lie all day in the baking sand
wondering where the shade of the cactus went.

PETRARCH'S WIFE

In a dreary suburban maisonette
the reincarnation of Petrarch's wife,
or the woman who should have been his wife,
has declared war on the sugared sonnet.

Instead of slender hands and long black hair
she's taken burnt-out cars and wheelie-bins,
and woven them with malicious care
into the Dublin prattle of her lines.

I called last night, but a message says:
"Too busy in the sonnet mines
to come to the phone right away,
but if you leave your name and fourteen lines,
or good rhymes for cider, condom, chip-van
I'll get back to you as soon as I can."

PANIC

*I had in mind a black dress I'd seen in Clery's
and the black boots I'd seen along Henry Street,
but I never made it, my lungs weren't up to it.
Or so I thought. Turned out later it was all
to do with iron deficiency and imagining the worst.*

On an ordinary Tuesday
I get off the bus
to die in my own bed;
and I was only
heading into town.
This breathing
makes life very difficult.

It has to do with long ago,
putting the dirty pearls
of rain into my mouth, neat…
off the windows the doors
the railings the steps
my mother's face;

a child imagining tears,
a woman holding them.

MOUNTAIN WOMAN

When he came home
I had crammed the garden
with cardboard boxes;
a neighbour had told me
they could break a fall.

I'd nets over the windows,
a trampoline out the back.
I clung to the kitchen door
and would not use the stairs.
I ditched my handbag and

began wearing a parachute.
When I sat, I sat on
cushions. When I slept,
I slept on a mattress
on the floor.

And then last night he asked,
"Are you expecting to fall?"
"Yes," I said, "I have been
climbing since I met you,
and it is a long way down.

Now the air is so thin
I am always afraid;
it is hard to breathe.
For the last few days
I've been clinging to this ledge.

But you see nothing,
all you do is moan about
a shambles of nets and boxes.
I used to think it was all
a question of balance.

That once I was tied to you
I'd be safe. When I'd climb,
you'd climb. When I fell,
you'd fall. But now I know
it is the fear of falling alone,

with nothing
or no one
to catch me,
that keeps me holding on,
and I need so much to let go."

JIMMY

For who can bear to feel himself forgotten.
W. H Auden

That old soldier,
he still comes round
every odd Tuesday afternoon.
He brings a glass eye,
a useless arm,
and all the war
that lingers on his skin;
a withered heart.
And yet, Jimmy
has the gentlest soul
I've ever known;
it's just he could never
climb out of the trench
they left him in.

These days he shuffles
when he walks
and his good hand shakes:
dampness gone to the bone.
Last night,
stroking my breasts,
he said the tips of my nipples
were smooth as bullets.
Then the air went silent,
as if we were waiting
for shells to fall,
I looked at him
sprawled naked,
a wounded man.
And I saw tears,
saw the glass-eye
like a sheet of ice
covering a flood.

THE OLYMPIANS

Next up are the poets.
This was never going
to be a glorious race
but after the pandemonium
of the heats
let's at least make sure
they're all facing the same way.

Running in lane one
in anonymous and fragments,
with a withered arm
and halt leg,
it's the Greek beauty Sappho,
all sandy smiles
and dark brown eyes,
it's rumoured
she moves like the wind

Beside her, in lane two,
with the haiku –
seventeen steps
of grace and precision –
it's the butterfly
of the short line,
representing Japan,
the little man, Basho.

In three with the sonnet
is William Shakespeare,
his run will depend
on impeccable rhythm,
on getting it all to flow.
Though a shadow is cast

over his selection
with Percy Shelley,
William Wordsworth,
Samuel Coleridge
and George Gordon, Lord Byron
all testing positive for opiates.

In lane four
with the villanelle
it's the Welshman Dylan Thomas:
after a lifetime of injuries
and unfulfilled promise
it's marvellous to see him
finally up on his feet.

In the middle of the field,
standing out like a king,
is the long-distance legend
blind Homer from Greece.
Kit Smart was a contender, but
he never turned up for the race.

Beside him,
crammed into six,
are Dante –
the Italian wizard,
the antelope of terza rima –
and a couple of farm boys,
Frost and Heaney.
I've seen them in practice,
they move with deceptive ease.
In lane seven, in the four
by four hundred relay,
it's the Russian champions –

they pass the baton
with silk-like grace –
Pasternak to Tsvetayeva,
Tsvetayeva to Mandelstam,
Mandelstam to Akhmatova.
She brings it home
with tremendous power
and gritty determination.

Out in lane eight,
going round the bend,
there's an army of poets.
I recognise at least a hundred
faces preparing for the start.

And then,
not with a shot
or a shout,
but with a collective sigh,
they're off.

It is poetry in motion,
like something out of Brueghel
the stillness is absolute,
for no one has moved.

They have closed their eyes
and are imagining
the wind on the faces
the sweat on the brow
the pain in the chest
the ache in the heart
the hardship
the loneliness
the grief
that has brought them to this.

Some are already
closing on the line.
Others will take
hours, days, weeks, months.
Some will still be running
when the crowds are gone
when the lights are off
when the stadium's closed

And some will
never make it home:
their words, their faces,
their lives forgotten.
They will turn to dust
where they fall.
The earth takes back
what it gives away –
the lanes run on forever.

NOW WINTER'S OVER

I've been told this winter's nearly over,
so I'd like to give thanks to you, O Lord,
and if not to you, than to whoever
led me through; for someone
kept me still under tumbling skies,
warm even on the darkest days.

Now, as she retreats, I watch her fold
her blanket of leaves in the field,
load her wagon with boxes of frost,
sheaves of ice, rolls of mist, barrels of rain.

Her last act will be
disposing of her enemies
caught like lambs in the briars –
the crows will pluck out their eyes.

From an open window
I'll watch green leaves
lick the blood from raindrops,
coax the life out of sunbeams,

suck till the smell of spring fills the air:
the cries of children in streets
the crackle of yellow crocuses
the eyes of leaves opening on trees.

If it weren't for the rest
of this dishevelled world,
I'd almost dare to say
I am happy to be alive.

FOUR REMEDIES

from *The Magical Book of Winter Cures*

1. Cure For The Broken Hearted

And this is the first of the healing cures,
the oldest remedy, the most often used –
it is of course for the broken hearted.
They come trailing clouds of dust,
their faces wet with tears. No excuses,
just an emptiness about them.
Beyond worry. The journey over.
They open their mouths and sip
like sinners seeking redemption;
then enter the darkness that I am.
In this room without walls, they bolt
the door, lie down and wait for the cure
to wash it all away: white as the winter sky.
A shower of hair over a pillow, a last memory.

The potion:

Seven days when no one calls.
Seven nights when nothing stirs.
Seven walks in the rain.
Seven ferocious prayers.
Seven gentle curses.
Seven lakes to swim in.
Seven woods to wander in.
Seven axes to cut away the wood.
Seven blades to cut away the skin.
Seven beds to toss in.

Seven master plans.
Seven panic attacks.
Seven circles of the asylum.
Seven hairs from the pillow.
Seven howls of rage.
Seven on seven on
Seven hours staring out the window.
Seven currachs ready for the voyage.
Seven bags of books.
Seven paintings.
Seven empty rooms.
Seven sleep filled nights.
Seven songs of thanks.

How to mix this cure,
where best to take it
depends on who you are.
I wonder if everything's here –
at its terrible cost,
I'd hate to think anything's lost.

2. Cure For Melancholia

This is one of the easiest cures,
though it's potent only a short while,
and sadly is not strong enough
to work on poets or painters
whose subject is the female nude.

Women should take it
when the moon is full.
Through I've heard the old say
it's best mixed in sunlight
or at least when there's
a break in the clouds.

First take a sprinkling
of river water from stretches
where the current is strong.
To this, add a few sloes,
a few blackberries,
one wild strawberry,
a little cinnamon. Next,

add a handful of grass
from an old hill fort
and a small bowl of nuts
from a hazel tree,
an orange
and a few raspberries –
for they are childhood.

To give the potion
a little lift,
add the blood of a swallow
and a feather from
its soft white breast.

Finally, squeeze the juice
from three yellow lemons.

Then take a clean round pot –
nothing with tin or aluminium –
and pour in a bottle of red wine.
Now heat over an open flame.

When the liquid begins to move
mix in the lot and stir and breathe
and stir and breathe and stir…
Strain, and drink before it cools.

Now sit by your fire
or better, lie in bed.

And if you share your life
with another weary soul,
stay off subjects such as
home improvements,
gardening,
children's education,
sexual satisfaction.

Stay in bed until
the weather changes,
take the cure
as often as necessary,
or until winter passes
your bit of the sky.

3. Cure For Excess Of Wine

Of all the ailments
in the world,
the love of drink
is the hardest to cure.

For, while wine cures
all the rest,
all the rest
lead back to red, red wine.

In older times
death by wine
was a fine death
for a poor poet.

Too good for them now
they rave on into old age
grey hair, grey words, supping
on a diet of bread and soup.

The craft is well again
so all is well,
no one watches
the door

for the swaying poet,
for the singing poet,
for the curse
of the poet…

The shame is gone.
The wine is sour,
but is that our loss
or the cure?

4. Cure For Loneliness

This is an old Russian cure,
better than a cup of tea,
more reliable than pills.
It was first formulated
by Leo Tolstoy in the
long winter of 1869.
A complex potion,
the recipe runs to 1,144 pages,
too long to put down here
but you'll find it on the creaking
shelves of any library
under the title *War and Peace*.

I suggest you take it
late at night,
beside an open fire,
with a map of old Russia
and a bottle of red wine.
I tried it myself
and it worked fine for me:
all the ghosts in my head
gathered round to hear
the tale of love and loss.

You could also try
some very old remedies
by Homer or Catullus,
or powerful ones
by Dante or Shakespeare,
or witches' brews
by Sappho or Tsvetayeva,
or complex Irish potions
by Messrs Joyce and Beckett.

Their cures hold a mirror up
to your soul – they work
incredibly well, though

I have found them addictive,
and the Beckett repeats
at odd times of the night.

These days
there is a whole
new range of panaceas:
heal-alls, cure-alls.
Some are like fire,
others like ice, but
none have been
tested by time.
However,
I do recommend,
for those darkest days,
the small healing potions
of Michael Hartnett.

Dublin born poet Tony Curtis is the author of four collections of poetry: *The Shifting of Stones* (1986), *Behind The Green Curtain* (1988), *This Far North* (1994) and *Three Songs Of Home* (1998). A member of Aosdána, the Irish academy of arts, and the recipient of the National Poetry Prize, he also edited *As the Poet Said* (1997). In 2003, he was awarded the Varuna House Exchange Fellowship to Australia.